W9-APJ-720

Team Spirit

THE PHILADELPHIA PHILLIES

BY
MARK STEWART

Content Consultant
James L. Gates, Jr.
Library Director
National Baseball Hall of Fame and Museum

NORWOOD HOUSE PRESS
CHICAGO, ILLINOIS

Norwood House Paperback Editions
An Imprint of Norwood House Press
P.O. Box 316598
Chicago, Illinois 60631
www.norwoodhousepress.com

For information regarding Norwood House Press, please visit our website at:
www.norwoodhousepress.com or call 866-565-2900.

All photos courtesy of Getty Images except the following:
F.W. Rueckheim & Brother (6, 21); DeLong Gum Co. (7);
Black Book archives (9 both, 22 bottom, 35 top and bottom left, 40 bottom);
Topps, Inc. (14, 22 top, 30, 37, 40 bottom left, 43); Mayo Brothers (20);
Classic Syndicate, Inc. (21 bottom); Bowman Gum Company (26, 41 bottom);
D. Buchner & Co. (29); Gum Inc. (34 top); Turkey Red (34 bottom left); Fatima (34 bottom right);
Author's collection (36, 41 top right); Select Publications, Inc. (40 top left);
TCMA Ltd. (41 bottom right). Cover photo by Drew Hallowell/Getty Images.
Special thanks to Topps, Inc.

Editor: Mike Kennedy
Designer: Ron Jaffe
Project Management: Black Book Partners, LLC.
Special thanks to Steve Hynes.

This book was manufactured as a paperback edition.
If you are purchasing this book as a rebound hardcover or without any cover,
the publisher and any licensors' rights are being violated.

Paperback ISBN: 978-1-60357-029-9

The Library of Congress has cataloged the original hardcover edition as follows:

Stewart, Mark, 1960-
   The Philadelphia Phillies / by Mark Stewart ; content consultant James L.
Gates.
      p. cm. -- (Team spirit)
   Summary: "Presents the history, accomplishments and key personalities of
the Philadelphia Phillies baseball team. Includes timelines, quotes, maps,
glossary and websites"--Provided by publisher.
   Includes bibliographical references and index.
   ISBN-13: 978-1-59953-171-7 (library edition : alk. paper)
   ISBN-10: 1-59953-171-2 (library edition : alk. paper)
   1. Philadelphia Phillies (Baseball team)--History--Juvenile literature. I.
Gates, James L. II. Title.
GV875.P45S74 2008
796.357'640974811--dc22
                                                                2007040057

© 2008 by Norwood House Press.
All rights reserved.
No part of this book may be reproduced without written permission from the publisher.

•

The Philadelphia Phillies is a registered trademark of The Phillies.
Major League Baseball trademarks and copyrights are used
with permission of Major League Baseball Properties, Inc.

Manufactured in the United States of America.

COVER PHOTO: The Phillies get ready to celebrate after a game-winning home run during the 2007 season.

Table of Contents

SPORTS WORDS & VOCABULARY WORDS: In this book, you will find many words that are new to you. You may also see familiar words used in new ways. The glossary on page 46 gives the meanings of baseball words, as well as "everyday" words that have special baseball meanings. These words appear in **bold type** throughout the book. The glossary on page 47 gives the meanings of vocabulary words that are not related to baseball. They appear in ***bold italic type*** throughout the book.

Meet the Phillies

The city of Philadelphia is known for its history, its hard-working people, and its love of sports. Only 11 other United States cities have professional baseball, basketball, hockey, and football. The Phillies are Philadelphia's oldest sports team. They have been bringing together friends, families, and baseball fans for more than 100 years.

In many ways, the Phillies are a reflection of the city. The players bring their talents from all over the world to live and work there. They feel the energy of the city and quickly become a part of its day-to-day life.

This book tells the story of the Phillies. They begin each season focused on baseball's highest prize. They play each game to win. When the Phillies take the field, the hearts of every baseball fan in Philadelphia go with them.

The Phillies celebrate after finishing in first place in 2007.

Way Back When

I n the earliest years of baseball, Philadelphia, Pennsylvania was one of the places where the game "grew up." People had been playing and watching the sport for a long time by the time the Phillies joined the **National League (NL)** in 1883. Over the next 125 years, the team would win the hearts of the fans—and sometimes drive them crazy.

ALEXANDER, PHILADELPHIA - NATIONALS

During the 1890s, the Phillies had some awesome teams and truly great players. Billy Hamilton, Ed Delahanty, and Sam Thompson formed an excellent outfield. Hamilton was baseball's greatest **leadoff hitter**. Delahanty was the game's most exciting **slugger**. Thompson had a strong bat and an even stronger throwing arm. Other stars of those early clubs were catcher Jack Clements, infielder Napoleon LaJoie, and pitcher Charlie Ferguson.

In the early 1900s, John Titus, Roy Thomas, and Sherry Magee gave the Phillies another excellent outfield. It was not until 1915, however, that the team won its first **pennant**. That club was led by a young pitching ace named Grover Cleveland Alexander. He, Erskine Mayer, and Eppa Rixey kept games close for Philadelphia's hitting stars, which included Gavvy Cravath, Dave Bancroft, and Fred Luderus.

The Phillies fell on hard times during the 1920s, 1930s, and 1940s. They had some great hitters—including Cy Williams and Chuck Klein—but the team played in a small ballpark, and their pitchers could not tame opposing hitters.

CHARLES (CHUCK) KLEIN
PHILADELPHIA NATIONALS

Finally, in 1950, the Phillies **assembled** a group of good young pitchers. Robin Roberts and Curt Simmons were two of the NL's best **starters**. Jim Konstanty was the league's top **relief pitcher**. With the help of young hitters Richie Ashburn, Del Ennis, Granny Hamner, and Willie "Puddin' Head" Jones, the Phillies won their second pennant. This group went down in baseball history as the "Whiz Kids."

More ups and downs followed, including the heartbreaking 1964 season, when the Phillies were in first place by a wide margin with 12 games to play. Unfortunately, they lost 10 in a row and finished tied for second.

LEFT: Grover Cleveland Alexander
ABOVE: Chuck Klein

Philadelphia fans were cheering again by the late 1970s. The Phillies had a great team led by hitting stars Mike Schmidt, Greg Luzinski, Bob Boone, Larry Bowa, and Garry Maddox. Their best pitcher was Steve Carlton. After Pete Rose joined the Phillies, they claimed pennants in 1980 and 1983, and won their first **World Series** in 1980.

In 1993, the Phillies returned to the World Series with a group of tough, lovable players. Darren Daulton, John Kruk, and Lenny Dykstra were the team leaders, along with pitching stars Curt Schilling and Mitch "Wild Thing" Williams. Although they fell just short of a second championship, that team captured the spirit of Philadelphia— and set the stage for all of the exciting baseball to come.

LEFT: Mike Schmidt, Pete Rose, and Larry Bowa, stars of the 1980 Phillies. **RIGHT**: Darren Daulton (top) and John Kruk (bottom), two of the leaders of the 1993 team.

The Team Today

The Phillies and their fans know what it takes to win a championship. Having a group of stars is a good start, but talent is not always enough. On a winning team, everyone must make a contribution.

The Phillies are at their best when they find the right mix of exciting young stars and older players with knowledge and experience. Starting in the 1990s, Philadelphia's **minor league system** began sending some very good players to the big leagues. Scott Rolen, Mike Lieberthal, Pat Burrell, Jimmy Rollins, Brett Myers, Chase Utley, Cole Hamels, and Ryan Howard became **All-Stars** with the Phillies. The challenge for the team is finding *experienced* players who are proven winners.

This challenge is what drives the Phillies. A winning record and **Most Valuable Player (MVP)** awards may look good on paper. But the team will not rest until it wins another championship on the field.

Ryan Howard is greeted by Shane Victorino and Jimmy Rollins after a home run in 2007. Howard and Rollins have both won the NL MVP award for the Phillies.

11

Home Turf

The Phillies spent 50 seasons in a ballpark known to most fans as the Baker Bowl. It fit neatly inside a rectangular city block. The left field fence was far away. The right field fence was 60 feet high but less than 300 feet from home plate. Fly balls that were easy outs in other cities were doubles, triples, and home runs in Philadelphia. The team's next stops were Connie Mack Stadium and Veterans Stadium.

In 2004, the Phillies moved into Citizens Bank Park. Like many modern stadiums, it mixes old and new building styles. One feature fans love is Ashburn Alley, which is named after **Hall of Famer** Richie Ashburn. It has souvenir shops and restaurants that make popular food, such as Philly cheesesteaks.

BY THE NUMBERS

- *The Phillies' stadium has 43,647 seats.*
- *The distance from home plate to the left field foul pole is 329 feet.*
- *The distance from home plate to the center field fence is 401 feet.*
- *The distance from home plate to the right field foul pole is 331 feet.*
- *In 2007, the stadium's food was voted #1 among all ballparks.*

The Phillies play the Atlanta Braves in Citizens Bank Park.

Dressed for Success

Since Philadelphia's "Whiz Kids" won the pennant in 1950, the main uniform color for the Phillies has been red. Before that, the team used combinations of red and blue—including some years with no red at all. In 1915, when the Phillies finished in first place for the first time, they wore red at home and blue on the road. They continued to do so for several seasons.

Since the 1930s, the team has almost always featured its name in one of two ways on its home uniforms. *Phillies* has either been spelled out in script, or a curly letter *P* has been used. During the

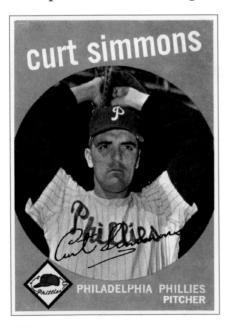

early 1940s, the team name was briefly changed to Blue Jays. The uniform still had Phillies on it, but a small blue jay patch was added to the sleeve. The new name never caught on, so the owners changed it back to Phillies. For nearly a century, the team's cap has also had the letter *P*.

Curt Simmons poses in the team's uniform from the 1950s.

UNIFORM BASICS

The baseball uniform has not changed much since the Phillies began playing. It has four main parts:

- a cap or batting helmet with a sun visor
- a top with a player's number on the back
- pants that reach down between the ankle and the knee
- stirrup-style socks

The uniform top sometimes has a player's name on the back. The team's name, city, or *logo* is usually on the front. Baseball teams wear light-colored uniforms when they play at home and darker styles when they play on the road.

For more than 100 years, baseball uniforms were made of wool *flannel* and were very baggy. This helped the sweat *evaporate* and gave players the freedom to move around. Today's uniforms are made of *synthetic* fabrics that stretch with players and keep them dry and cool.

Cole Hamels wears Philadelphia's 2007 home uniform.

We Won!

The Phillies began their 98th year with high hopes but low expectations. Their fans knew the 1980 team had a good chance to win the pennant. They were also used to the club *folding* when the pressure was on.

Philadelphia's leader in 1980 was Pete Rose, who had won two championships with the Cincinnati Reds. The team's best pitcher was Steve Carlton, who won 24 times that year. Their top hitter was Mike Schmidt, the NL's home run champion. Their relief ace was Tug McGraw, who threw a twisting **screwball** that was almost impossible to hit.

As spring turned to summer and summer turned to fall, Philadelphia fans did what they always did—cheered, booed, and

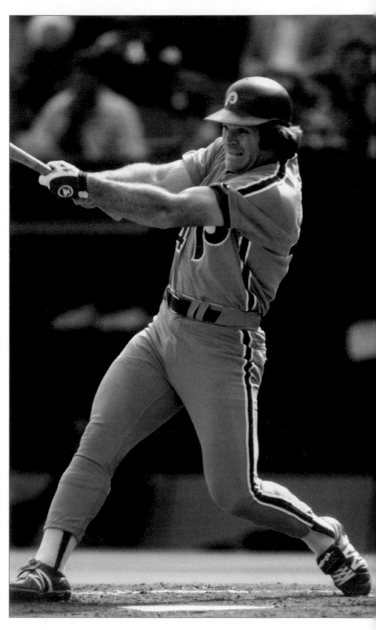

LEFT: Mike Schmidt
RIGHT: Pete Rose

hoped for the best for the Phillies. There seemed to be something different about this team. In the last few weeks, the players pulled together and caught the first-place Montreal Expos. Schmidt smashed a home run against them in the next-to-last game, and the Phillies won the **NL East**.

Carlton beat the Houston Astros in the first game of the **National League Championship Series (NLCS)**. The next four games were all decided in **extra innings**. It was the most exciting pennant battle in history. In the final game, the Astros led 5–2 in the eighth inning, but the Phillies made a great *comeback*. They won 8–7 on a 10th inning hit by Garry Maddox.

The Phillies faced the Kansas City Royals in the World Series. The first five games were very close. Philadelphia won the first two at home, and the Royals won the next two after the series moved to Kansas City.

The Royals were ahead in the ninth inning of Game Five, but Philadelphia's Del Unser stroked a **pinch-hit** double to drive in the tying run. Moments later, he scored the winning run. Instead of being behind by a game, Philadelphia moved ahead by a game and took a big advantage in the series.

In Game Six, Carlton won for the second time against Kansas City. McGraw replaced him in the eighth inning and worked out of two bases-loaded situations. Thanks to McGraw's great relief work, the Phillies survived to win their first championship. Schmidt, who hit two homers and drove in seven runs, was named the series MVP.

ABOVE: Steve Carlton pitches against the Kansas City Royals in the 1980 World Series.   **RIGHT**: Tug McGraw jumps for joy after the final out of Game Six.

Go-To Guys

To be a true star in baseball, you need more than a quick bat and a strong arm. You have to be a "go-to guy"—someone the manager wants on the pitcher's mound or in the batter's box when it matters most. Fans of the Phillies have had a lot to cheer about over the years, including these great stars …

THE PIONEERS

ED DELAHANTY   Outfielder

- BORN: 10/30/1867   • DIED: 7/2/1903
- PLAYED FOR TEAM: 1888 TO 1889 & 1891 TO 1901

Pitchers hated throwing to Ed Delahanty. He would swing at any ball at any time, and he usually hit it a long way.

GROVER CLEVELAND ALEXANDER   Pitcher

- BORN: 2/26/1887   • DIED: 11/4/1950
- PLAYED FOR TEAM: 1911 TO 1917 & 1930

Grover Cleveland Alexander was called "Pete" by teammates and fans in Philadelphia. He had a sinking fastball and a sharp-breaking curveball. Alexander led the NL in wins five times with the Phillies. He set a record for **rookies** with 28 victories in 1911.

ABOVE: Ed Delahanty
TOP RIGHT: Gavvy Cravath   **BOTTOM RIGHT**: Richie Ashburn

GAVVY CRAVATH   Outfielder

- BORN: 3/23/1881   • DIED: 5/23/1963   • PLAYED FOR TEAM: 1912 TO 1920

When Gavvy Cravath played, the right field fence in the Phillies' ballpark was very close to home plate. Though he was a right-handed hitter, Cravath learned how to smash balls to the opposite field. He led the NL in home runs six times.

CHUCK KLEIN   Outfielder

- BORN: 10/7/1904   • DIED: 3/28/1958
- PLAYED FOR TEAM: 1928 TO 1933 & 1936 TO 1944

CRAVATH, PHILADELPHIA - NATIONALS

Chuck Klein also knew how to use Philadelphia's tiny ballpark. He was a powerful left-handed hitter who led the NL in home runs four times and won the **Triple Crown** in 1933.

ROBIN ROBERTS   Pitcher

- BORN: 9/30/1926   • PLAYED FOR TEAM: 1948 TO 1961

Robin Roberts threw hard and had very good control. He led the NL in wins four years in a row and in strikeouts twice. Roberts pitched more than 300 innings six times.

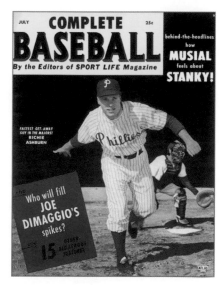

RICHIE ASHBURN   Outfielder

- BORN: 3/19/1927   • DIED: 9/9/1997
- PLAYED FOR TEAM: 1948 TO 1959

Richie Ashburn was one of the best defensive players in history. He was a good hitter, too. Ashburn led the league in batting twice.

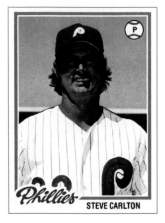

STEVE CARLTON
STEVE CARLTON

STEVE CARLTON   Pitcher

• BORN: 12/22/1944   • PLAYED FOR TEAM: 1972 TO 1986

Steve Carlton had an excellent fastball, curveball, and slider—a pitch that bent and dipped sharply right before it reached home plate. In 1972, the Phillies finished last, but Carlton finished first in the NL in wins, strikeouts, and **earned run average (ERA)**. He led the Phillies to the pennant in 1980 and won two games in the World Series.

MIKE SCHMIDT   Third Baseman

• BORN: 9/27/1949   • PLAYED FOR TEAM: 1972 TO 1989

Mike Schmidt was the greatest slugger ever to play third base. He was also one of the best fielders. Schmidt led the league in home runs eight

times and won 10 **Gold Glove** awards. He was named the NL MVP three times in the 1980s.

CURT SCHILLING   Pitcher

• BORN: 11/14/1966   • PLAYED FOR TEAM: 1992 TO 2000

Curt Schilling was one of baseball's *fiercest competitors*. After leading the Phillies to the pennant in 1993, he suffered an arm injury. He changed his pitching style and came back to lead the NL in strikeouts in 1997 and 1998.

JIMMY ROLLINS — Shortstop

- BORN: 11/27/1978   • FIRST YEAR WITH TEAM: 2000

Jimmy Rollins was the league's stolen base champion in his first full year with the Phillies. His speed, power, and great fielding quickly made him one of the most exciting players the team ever had. In 2007, he won the NL MVP award.

CHASE UTLEY — Second Baseman

- BORN: 12/17/1978   • FIRST YEAR WITH TEAM: 2003

In college, Chase Utley was one of the best hitters ever. When he joined the Phillies, he kept on hitting. Utley led the NL in runs scored in 2006 and was third in the league in batting in 2007.

RYAN HOWARD — First Baseman

- BORN: 11/19/1979   • FIRST YEAR WITH TEAM: 2004

In 2005, Ryan Howard was asked to fill in for Philadelphia's injured slugger Jim Thome. He hit 22 home runs in 88 games and was voted NL **Rookie of the Year**. One season later, Howard hit 58 home runs and was named league MVP.

TOP LEFT: Steve Carlton
BOTTOM LEFT: Curt Schilling
TOP RIGHT: Jimmy Rollins
BOTTOM RIGHT: Ryan Howard

On the Sidelines

The Phillies have had some of baseball's greatest managers. In the 1880s, Harry Wright ran the club. Wright was a legend in baseball—he had put together the first professional team in 1869. Another early manager was Pat Moran. His players practiced the *fundamentals* of baseball over and over until they were almost perfect. Moran's club won the pennant in 1915.

Danny Ozark and Dallas Green managed the Phillies in the 1970s and early 1980s. They both had short tempers and were hard on their players, but the team reached the **playoffs** five times and won a World Series during that period.

In 1983, Paul Owens went from Philadelphia's business office to the dugout. He traded his coat and tie for the manager's uniform in the middle of the year. He let the older players lead the younger ones, and the Phillies returned to the World Series. Ten seasons later, Jim Fregosi led the Phillies from last place to first place. Under Fregosi, Philadelphia won its fifth pennant.

Charlie Manuel followed in the footsteps of other great Philadelphia managers when he led the team to the NL East crown in 2007.

One Great Day

When the Phillies took the field on the last day of the 1950 season, they were trying to do something no Philadelphia team had done in 35 seasons—win the pennant. Their opponent was the Brooklyn Dodgers. The two teams faced each other in Brooklyn's Ebbets Field. If the Phillies won, they were NL champions. If the Dodgers won, a playoff series would decide the pennant.

DICK SISLER

Robin Roberts was the starting pitcher for the Phillies. It was his fourth game in eight days. Don Newcombe pitched for the Dodgers. Each starter had 19 wins and wanted number 20 badly. Both were at their best from the first pitch. Newcombe gave up a run in the top of the sixth inning, and Roberts gave up a run in the bottom of the sixth.

The Dodgers nearly won the game in the ninth. Duke Snider hit a single with Cal Abrams on second base. Richie Ashburn was playing

26

LEFT: Dick Sisler, whose home run beat the Brooklyn Dodgers.
RIGHT: Robin Roberts, the winning pitcher that day.

shallow in center field, and he threw a strike to home plate. Abrams was tagged out by catcher Stan Lopata. The Dodgers then loaded the bases, but Roberts got two pop-outs to end the inning.

In the top of the 10th, Dick Sisler came to bat. He was known by many fans as the son of George Sisler, a great hitter who made it into the Hall of Fame. Moments later, Dick made some history of his own. He belted a three-run home run off Newcombe to give the Phillies a 4–1 lead.

Though he was near exhaustion, Roberts set down all three Brooklyn hitters in the bottom of the 10th. Philadelphia's "Whiz Kids" won the pennant, and Roberts became the first pitcher to win 20 games for the Phillies since 1917.

"You did it!" shouted Lopata.

"I couldn't have gone much further," Roberts admitted.

Legend Has It

Who was the unluckiest Phillies fan?

LEGEND HAS IT that Alice Roth was. During a 1957 game, a foul ball by Richie Ashburn hit her in the nose. The game was stopped, and Alice was placed on a stretcher. When the game *resumed*, Ashburn fouled off another pitch—and hit Alice again!

ABOVE: Richie Ashburn, who was known for fouling off a lot of pitches.
RIGHT: Jack Clements, in a trading card from his days with the Phillies.

28

How did the Phillies save money on cutting their grass in their early years?

LEGEND HAS IT that they used sheep. After William Baker bought the team in 1911, he kept a herd of sheep under the stands. They would come out and clip the grass when it got too long. This plan lasted until 1925, when a ram ***butted*** the team's secretary. That finally convinced Baker to buy a lawnmower.

Who was the best left-handed catcher in history?

LEGEND HAS IT that Jack Clements was. Lefty catchers are a rare thing in baseball. There have only been a few in history. That is because most batters are right-handed, which means a left-handed catcher has to throw "over" the batter more often. Also, left-handers with strong arms usually end up as pitchers. Clements was a

CLEMENTS, CATCHER, PHILA.

short, powerful man with a good batting eye and a quick, accurate throwing motion. He hit .394 in 1895—the highest average ever for a catcher.

It Really Happened

The Phillies and Chicago Cubs have played some wild games over the years. The wildest came on a windy day early in the 1976 season at Chicago's Wrigley Field. After three innings, the Cubs were ahead 12–1. Philadelphia manager Danny Ozark had already sent pitchers Steve Carlton, Ron Schueler, and Gene Garber to the showers.

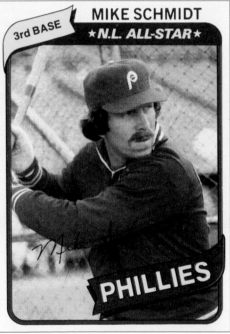

When Mike Schmidt stepped into the batter's box with a runner on base in the fifth inning, little had changed. The score was 13–2. Chicago starter Rick Reuschel delivered a pitch, and the Phillies' slugger hit a two-run homer. Schmidt came up again in the seventh inning and hit another home run off Reuschel. It made the score 13–7.

One inning later, Schmidt hit his third home run of the game. It came off Mike Garman and brought the Phillies to within a run, at 13–12. Philadelphia continued its comeback and moved ahead 15–13 in the ninth inning, but Chicago fought back to tie the game.

Extra innings meant that Schmidt would bat again. He faced Paul Reuschel (Rick's brother) with a runner on first. Schmidt cracked his fourth home run of the day. He joined Ed Delahanty and Chuck Klein as the only Phillies to hit that many in one game.

Amazingly, the scoring was not done. Each team **plated** one more run that afternoon, but the Phillies held on for a *remarkable* 18–16 victory.

LEFT: A trading card shows slugger Mike Schmidt during batting practice.
ABOVE: Schmidt bats against the Chicago Cubs in Wrigley Field.

Team Spirit

The word "fan" is short for *fanatic*. Philadelphia baseball fans are known for being loud and emotional when they are at the stadium. During the 1977 playoffs, they were so loud that an opposing pitcher could not concentrate. His manager had to take him out of the game.

The very next spring, the team *unveiled* its new *mascot*, the Phillie Phanatic. It replaced Phil and Phillis. They were a brother and sister who dressed in old-time uniforms. The Phanatic is bright green. It looks a little like a *gigantic* Sesame Street Muppet. It has been voted the best mascot in baseball.

No one knows what the Phanatic will do next. Often it dances in front of the visiting team's dugout and teases the players. Sometimes before games, the Phanatic will steal a fielder's glove and throw it into the stands. When there is a break in the action, the Phanatic hops on an ATV and drives around the ballpark. Philadelphia fans adore their Phanatic.

The Phillie Phanatic entertains the crowd.

Timeline

Chuck
Klein

1883
The Phillies join the
National League.

1933
Chuck Klein wins
the Triple Crown.

1910
Sherry Magee wins the
NL batting championship.

1915
The Phillies win
their first pennant.

1950
The "Whiz Kids"
win the NL pennant.

Sherry
Magee

A team photo of
the Phillies from
the early 1900s.

Curt Schilling, the top pitcher on the 1993 team.

1972
Steve Carlton wins the NL **Cy Young Award**.

1993
The Phillies reach the World Series for the fifth time.

2002
Bobby Abreu leads the NL with 50 doubles.

1964
Johnny Callison wins the **All-Star Game** with a home run.

1980
The Phillies defeat the Kansas City Royals to win the World Series.

2006
Ryan Howard wins the Home Run Derby and NL MVP award.

Tug McGraw, one of the heroes of the 1980 team.

Ryan Howard bats during the Home Run Derby.

Fun Facts

EYE ON THE SKY

During the 1930s, the Phillies did not draw many fans to the ballpark.

They did everything to get attention—including trying to catch a ball thrown from the top of a downtown office building.

LONG TOSS

Glen Gorbous may have had the strongest arm in history. In 1957, the Philadelphia outfielder threw a ball 445 feet, 10 inches on the fly.

STREAKIN'

In 1899, Ed Delahanty set a team record by hitting safely in 31 games in a row. That record stood for 106 years until Jimmy Rollins broke it in 2006 with a 38-game hitting streak. That same season, Chase Utley made a run at the mark. He got a hit in 35 games in a row.

DOING IT ALL

In 1971, Rick Wise became the only pitcher to throw a **no-hitter** and hit two home runs in the same game.

JUAN–DERFUL

From 1984 to 1987, Juan Samuel was the only **major leaguer** to hit 10 or more doubles, triples, and home runs in each season.

NICE GOING, DAD

Jim Bunning had quite a Father's Day in 1964. He pitched a no-hitter against the New York Mets! Later in life, Bunning became a U.S. senator.

COMEBACK KINGS

In 2007, the Phillies were seven games behind the Mets with 17 games left to play. They caught fire and won the NL East. No team had ever made up so many games so late in the season.

LEFT: The Phillies prepare to catch a ball thrown off a building in 1939.
ABOVE: Jim Bunning

Talking Baseball

"Any time you think you have the game **conquered**, the game will turn around and punch you in the nose."

> —*Mike Schmidt, on respecting the game of baseball*

"If I just go out and play, the rest will take care of itself. That's what my parents taught me. They haven't been wrong yet."

> —*Ryan Howard, on keeping your focus as a big leaguer*

"Physical ability only goes so far. You have to work hard the rest of the way."

> —*Jimmy Rollins, on why he does not rely only on his natural talent*

"I never want to look in the mirror and say, 'What if? What if I had run harder? What if I had dived for that ground ball?'"

—*Chase Utley, on why he never gives up on a play*

"With all the **glamour** attached to hitting the ball out of the park, it takes a lot of discipline to go up there and just try to get a base hit."

—*Garry Maddox, on being a singles hitter*

"It may be a silly thing to say, but honestly, I actually don't think too much when I'm out there on the mound."

—*Robin Roberts, on pitching with a 95 mile-per-hour fastball*

LEFT: Ryan Howard
ABOVE: Garry Maddox

For the Record

The great Phillies teams and players have left their marks on the record books. These are the "best of the best" …

PHILLIES AWARD WINNERS

WINNER	AWARD	YEAR
Chuck Klein	Most Valuable Player	1933
Jim Konstanty	Most Valuable Player	1950
Jack Sanford	Rookie of the Year	1957
Johnny Callison	All-Star Game MVP	1964
Richie Allen	Rookie of the Year	1964
Steve Carlton	Cy Young Award	1972
Steve Carlton	Cy Young Award	1977
Steve Carlton	Cy Young Award	1980
Mike Schmidt	Most Valuable Player	1980
Mike Schmidt	World Series MVP	1980
Mike Schmidt	Most Valuable Player	1981
Steve Carlton	Cy Young Award	1982
John Denny	Cy Young Award	1983
Mike Schmidt	Most Valuable Player	1986
Steve Bedrosian	Cy Young Award	1987
Scott Rolen	Rookie of the Year	1997
Larry Bowa	Manager of the Year	2001
Ryan Howard	Rookie of the Year	2005
Ryan Howard	Most Valuable Player	2006
Jimmy Rollins	Most Valuable Player	2007

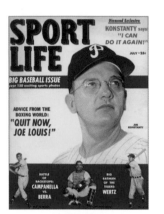

Jim Konstanty

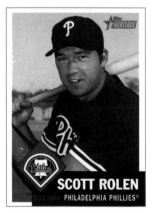

Scott Rolen

Mike Schmidt at his Hall of Fame ceremony.

PHILLIES ACHIEVEMENTS

ACHIEVEMENT	YEAR
NL Pennant Winners	1915
NL Pennant Winners	1950
NL East Champions	1976
NL East Champions	1977
NL East Champions	1978
NL East Champions	1980
NL Pennant Winners	1980
World Series Champions	1980
NL East First-Half Champions*	1981
NL East Champions	1983
NL Pennant Winners	1983
NL East Champions	1993
NL Pennant Winners	1993
NL East Champions	2007

The 1981 season was played with first-half and second-half division winners.

PUDDIN' HEAD JONES

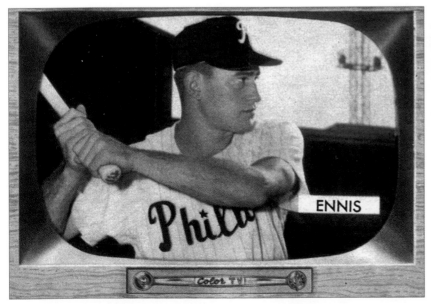

Del Ennis (**LEFT**) and Willie Jones (**ABOVE**), stars of the 1950 team.
TOP: A 1993 yearbook autographed by Curt Schilling.

Pinpoints

The history of a baseball team is made up of many smaller stories. These stories take place all over the map—not just in the city a team calls "home." Match the pushpins on these maps to the Team Facts and you will begin to see the story of the Phillies unfold!

TEAM FACTS

1. Philadelphia, Pennsylvania—*The Phillies have played here since 1883.*
2. Strykersville, New York—*Jim Konstanty was born here.*
3. Dayton, Ohio—*Mike Schmidt was born here.*
4. Chicago, Illinois—*Greg Luzinski was born here.*
5. Elba, Nebraska—*Grover Cleveland Alexander was born here.*
6. Qualls, Oklahoma—*Johnny Callison was born here.*
7. Miami, Florida—*Steve Carlton was born here.*
8. Pasadena, California—*Chase Utley was born here.*
9. Sacramento, California—*Larry Bowa was born here.*
10. Anchorage, Alaska—*Curt Schilling was born here.*
11. Maracay, Venezuela—*Bobby Abreu was born here.*
12. San Pedro de Macoris, Dominican Republic—*Juan Samuel was born here.*

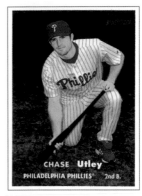

Chase Utley

Play Ball

Baseball is a game played between two teams over nine innings. Teams take one turn at bat and one turn in the field during each inning. A turn at bat ends when three outs are made. The batters on the hitting team try to reach base safely. The players on the fielding team try to prevent this from happening.

In baseball, the ball is controlled by the pitcher. The pitcher must throw the ball to the batter, who decides whether or not to swing at each pitch. If a batter swings and misses, it is a strike. If the batter lets a good pitch go by, it is also a strike. If the batter swings and the ball does not stay in fair territory (between the v-shaped lines that begin at home plate) it is called "foul," and is counted as a strike. If the pitcher throws three strikes, the batter is out. If the pitcher throws four bad pitches before that, the batter is awarded first base. This is called a base-on-balls, or "walk."

When the batter swings the bat and hits the ball, everyone springs into action. If a fielder catches a batted ball before it hits the ground, the batter is out. If a fielder scoops the ball off the ground and throws it to first base before the batter arrives, the batter is out. If the batter reaches first base safely, he is credited with a hit. A one-base hit is called a single, a two-base hit is called a double, a three-base hit is called a triple, and a four-base hit is called a home run.

Runners who reach base are only safe when they are touching one of the bases. If they are caught between the bases, the fielders can tag them with the ball and record an out.

A batter who is able to circle the bases and make it back to home plate before three outs are made is credited with a run scored. The team with the most runs after nine innings is the winner.

Anyone who has played baseball (or softball) knows that it can be a complicated game. Every player on the field has a job to do. Different players have different strengths and weaknesses. The pitchers, batters, and managers make hundreds of decisions every game. The more you play and watch baseball, the more "little things" you are likely to notice. The next time you are at a game, look for these plays:

PLAY LIST

DOUBLE PLAY—A play where the fielding team is able to make two outs on one batted ball. This usually happens when a runner is on first base, and the batter hits a ground ball to one of the infielders. The base runner is forced out at second base and the ball is then thrown to first base before the batter arrives.

HIT AND RUN—A play where the runner on first base sprints to second base while the pitcher is throwing the ball to the batter. When the second baseman or shortstop moves toward the base to wait for the catcher's throw, the batter tries to hit the ball to the place that the fielder has just left. If the batter swings and misses, the fielding team can tag the runner out.

INTENTIONAL WALK—A play when the pitcher throws four bad pitches on purpose, allowing the batter to walk to first base. This happens when the pitcher would much rather face the next batter—and is willing to risk putting a runner on base.

SACRIFICE BUNT—A play where the batter makes an out on purpose so that a teammate can move to the next base. On a bunt, the batter tries to "deaden" the pitch with the bat instead of swinging at it.

SHOESTRING CATCH—A play where an outfielder catches a short hit an inch or two above the ground, near the tops of his shoes. It is not easy to run as fast as you can and lower your glove without slowing down. It can be risky, too. If a fielder misses a shoestring catch, the ball might roll all the way to the fence.

Glossary

BASEBALL WORDS TO KNOW

ALL-STAR GAME—Baseball's annual game featuring the best players from the American League and National League.

ALL-STARS—Players who are selected to play in baseball's annual All-Star Game.

CY YOUNG AWARD—The annual trophy given to each league's best pitcher.

EARNED RUN AVERAGE (ERA)—A statistic that counts how many runs a pitcher gives up for every nine innings he pitches.

EXTRA INNINGS—Innings played when a game is tied after nine innings.

GOLD GLOVE—An award given each year to baseball's best fielders.

HALL OF FAMER—A player honored in baseball's Hall of Fame, a museum in Cooperstown, New York.

LEADOFF HITTER—The first hitter in a lineup, or the first hitter in an inning.

MAJOR LEAGUER—Someone who plays in either the American League or National League, which make up today's major leagues.

MINOR LEAGUE SYSTEM—An organization set up by a big-league team. The club develops young players in this system.

MOST VALUABLE PLAYER (MVP)—An award given each year to each league's top player; an MVP is also selected for the World Series and All-Star Game.

NATIONAL LEAGUE (NL)—The older of the two major leagues; the NL began play in 1876 and the American League (AL) started in 1901.

NATIONAL LEAGUE CHAMPIONSHIP SERIES (NLCS)—The competition that has decided the National League pennant since 1969.

NL EAST—A group of National League teams that plays in the eastern part of the country.

NO-HITTER—A game in which a team is unable to get a hit.

PENNANT—A league championship. The term comes from the triangular flag awarded to each season's champion, beginning in the 1870s.

PINCH-HIT—Taking a teammate's turn to hit.

PLATED—Scored or drove home.

PLAYOFFS—The games played after the regular season to determine which teams will advance to the World Series.

RELIEF PITCHER—A pitcher who is brought into a game to replace another pitcher. Relief pitchers can be seen warming up in the bullpen.

ROOKIE OF THE YEAR—The annual award given to each league's best first-year player.

ROOKIES—Players in their first season.

SCREWBALL—A pitch that darts in the opposite direction of a curveball.

SLUGGER—A powerful hitter.

STARTERS—Pitchers who begin the game for their team.

TRIPLE CROWN—An honor given to a player who leads the league in home runs, batting average, and runs batted in.

WORLD SERIES—The world championship series played between the winners of the National League and American League.

OTHER WORDS TO KNOW

ASSEMBLED—Put together.

BUTTED—Struck with the head or horns.

COMEBACK—The process of catching up from behind, or making up a large deficit.

COMPETITORS—People who have a strong desire to win.

CONQUERED—Gained full advantage.

EVAPORATE—Disappear, or turn into vapor.

EXPERIENCED—Having knowledge and skill in a job.

FANATIC—A person who is excessively devoted to someone or something.

FIERCEST—Most aggressive.

FLANNEL—A soft wool or cotton material.

FOLDING—Failing or collapsing.

FUNDAMENTALS—The most basic parts of something.

GIGANTIC—Huge.

GLAMOUR—Excitement and charm.

LOGO—A symbol or design that represents a company or team.

MASCOT—An animal or person believed to bring a group good luck.

REMARKABLE—Unusual or exceptional.

RESUMED—Began again after a break.

SYNTHETIC—Made in a laboratory, not in nature.

UNVEILED—Made public.

Places to Go

ON THE ROAD

PHILADELPHIA PHILLIES
One Citizens Bank Way
Philadelphia, Pennsylvania 19148
(215) 463-6000

**NATIONAL BASEBALL
HALL OF FAME AND MUSEUM**
25 Main Street
Cooperstown, New York 13326
(888) 425-5633
www.baseballhalloffame.org

ON THE WEB

THE PHILADELPHIA PHILLIES   www.philadelphiaphillies.com
  • *Learn more about the Phillies*

MAJOR LEAGUE BASEBALL   www.mlb.com
  • *Learn more about all the major league teams*

MINOR LEAGUE BASEBALL   www.minorleaguebaseball.com
  • *Learn more about the minor leagues*

ON THE BOOKSHELF

To learn more about the sport of baseball, look for these books at your library or bookstore:

  • Kelly, James. *Baseball*. New York, New York: DK, 2005.

  • Jacobs, Greg. *The Everything Kids' Baseball Book*. Cincinnati, Ohio: Adams Media Corporation, 2006.

  • Stewart, Mark and Kennedy, Mike. *Long Ball: The Legend and Lore of the Home Run*. Minneapolis, Minnesota: Millbrook Press, 2006.

Index

PAGE NUMBERS IN **BOLD** REFER TO ILLUSTRATIONS.

The Team

MARK STEWART has written more than 25 books on baseball, and over 100 sports books for kids. He grew up in New York City during the 1960s rooting for the Yankees and Mets, and now takes his two daughters, Mariah and Rachel, to the same ball-parks. Mark comes from a family of writers. His grand-father was Sunday Editor of the *New York Times* and his mother was Articles Editor of *Ladies' Home Journal* and *McCall's*. Mark has profiled hundreds of athletes over the last 20 years. He has also written several books about his native New York and New Jersey, his home today. Mark is a graduate of Duke University, with a degree in history. He lives with his daughters and wife, Sarah, overlooking Sandy Hook, NJ.

JAMES L. GATES, JR. has served as Library Director at the National Baseball Hall of Fame since 1995. He had previously served in academic libraries for almost fifteen years. He holds degrees from Belmont Abbey College, the University of Notre Dame, and Indiana University. During his career Jim has authored several aca-demic articles and has served in an editorial capacity on multiple book, mag-azine, and museum publications, and he also serves as host for  the Annual Cooperstown Symposium on Baseball and American Culture. He is an ardent Baltimore Orioles fan and enjoys watching baseball with his wife and two children.